TRUFFLE BEDS

Katherine Pierpoint

faber and faber

LONDON · BOSTON

First published in 1995
by Faber and Faber Limited
3 Queen Square London WC1N 3AU

Photoset in Linotype Sabon by Wilmaset Ltd, Wirral
Printed in England by Clays Ltd, St Ives plc

© Katherine Pierpoint, 1995

Katherine Pierpoint is hereby identified as author of this work in
accordance with Section 77 of the Copyright, Designs and
Patents Act 1988

A CIP record for this book
is available from the British Library

ISBN 0–571–17360–8

2 4 6 8 10 9 7 5 3 1

To one and all

Acknowledgements

My thanks to the Hawthornden Castle International Retreat for Writers for the Fellowship awarded in 1993 and to Christopher Reid for his encouragement. I am also grateful to the editors of *Frogmore Papers*, *The New Yorker*, *The Rialto* and *Vision On*, and to the judges of the Arvon International Poetry Competition 1991, the Charterhouse International Poetry Competition 1992, the SKOOB/ Index on Censorship International Poetry Competition 1992 and the Sidmouth Arts Festival Open Poetry Competition 1993.

Contents

The Twist in the River

At the clear, beer-coloured and bubbleshot twist in the river —
Every stone a speckled egg spawned in that deep lap,
Every pockmarked, pitted pebble a planet, blindly seeing through its
   own evolution —
The shallows, and the tall air, are filled with sound and light.
This part of the river expects to be seen, for it has drawn you there,
And the trees, selfless, introduce the sky into your love for the water.
If this place were a person, it would be making up a paper hat while
   humming,
Entirely self-contained, absorbed yet radiant —
A family moment, appearing normal until years later in retrospect,
When its depths are fully felt, beyond blunt experience.

Underwater, the light thickens slightly but never sets
And the river runs through its own fingers, careless.

Goatfall

The nanny goats ripple from the stables into sudden morning sun,
Odd wisps of broken clover straw still clinging to their bags and
    bellies;
A jerky, circumspect stepping, blinking pinkly at the sun and
    adjusting their bite,
Then chiming down the track in a cloud of leather and ammonia.

Once they have streamed away
The man crosses the yard to fetch the old male goat from the end
    shed,
Always in dripping green shade under the trees.
A gamey goat breath fills that deep hole;
The man halts a moment, turns aside and wipes his own mouth.

They set off up the track, past dirt-bathing hens.
Sunlight does not become the goat in his iron chain,
An idiot twitch and rattle rambling along his ridged back.
The goat picks his way ahead, all black rags and bone.
Legs thinner than a peeled stick
Leave twin kidney marks in the mud.
He goes lipping at the newest growths,
The delicate buddings, and
The filthy garlic herbs, mandrake; eldritch . . .

How far he can swing into the hedge for buds too high for the
    nannies,
Dabbing at the bread-and-cheese of hawthorn
With thin, warm lips on a raw steel beak.

That head – how close the warm bone lies to the surface –
Like touching the rocking, topmost stone of a cairn which may fall.

In him is an arsenal of chipped and horn-ringed tough years,
Red and black history of much fighting;
Triangular springing to clash heads.
A memory stirs of a boiling March anger, the rattling leap and then
Some mighty unseen hand that chopped hard in from behind
To rip him back in mid-flight,
Plucked a single terrible note on his chain and sucked away his air,
Choking and strangling,
Then dangled him high
To smash down on his knees
With the windrush and roar of a falling tree.

The memory turns him; he edges round, lays his head flat,
Cheek down on the air like an intent listener;
Climbs high on a log laid by the hedge,
Tries to get all the world behind his head,
Ready to swing and ram its deepest meat.

Then another plan stings.
With one acid eye holding out against the may-tree
Where a blackbird screams into bosomy blossom,
He rears up from the carefully chosen log plinth,
Clawing his front legs up the whirling sky,
And falls forwards –
Hurtling black enormous shape quicker than a shock, forelegs high
To use the deep ribcage to knock the man flat;
A rank meteor
In rampant declension,
Stink of sour piss on his belly.

The man steps aside and grabs a horn as it slices by;
Holds it hard at the deep root into the skull where dark marrow starts,

Twists back and lays the old head flat along the neck
To lie mute on the shoulders.
Throat exposed, eyes full of fear and hate,
The goat freezes now, as he can't see down;
Cannot trust his feet, the world.
Must tiptoe on the cracking icefloes of hated guidance.

They start the path home under the arching trees, each leaning into
the other.

Boats

Out in the estuary the skywater's all unravelled and gone away.
It left one pale and dibbled curl,
Twined on a porous skin-curd that works in sleep.

A sighing, ticking, supping everywhere
Of many blind bubblemouths held upturned to the air,
Timeless wattle-and-daubing
In the pith beneath the ringed mudflats.

The boats were last seen bobbing
With the comfortable, tiny mind of pigeons.
They wait now, immobile at dangerous angles.
Stuntmen clinging while the actress,
So beautiful she invents her own law daily,
Leaves the set, unannounced.
Cool mother of pearl, gone secret tigering elsewhere.

This open loss of the boats' level ease!
They're a wooden herd of pregnant flanks now, ribs pushed up and out.
Some, cocked high, listen with their entire bodies
For the first signal of remembrance from the sea;
Others in the dwindling channel slowly point in many directions at once,
Stiff fingers seeking old patterns on piano keys.
Walrus elders napping, one-buttocked on the unforgiving pew.

A smell of green-black gas bites on the recoiling tongue.

Ancient sailors, maddened by months in a queasy, migrant prison,
The ripping sloughs of salt-stiffened skin, the damp and rancid bunks –
A worse state yet than marriage, in their trestle-thumping brags –

Once swarmed ashore to stake a claim to new land.
One, planning already that the ugly but virgin island
Should bear his name alone,
Smashed the first great cratering blow to the stake,
High on rum and violence;
And, screaming, found the cockle-studded shore
Shot forth leviathan blood
And the land, roaring, suddenly sunk like the stone it was not.

In the Outhouse

Staying with a friend, you leave his mother's kitchen,
To walk the garden on an errand for herbs.
The wind snaps the drying sheets apart on the washing line
Giving sudden, triangular glimpses of a pond, and roses.

And here's an outhouse, with a scrap of frayed rush matting on the
    red step;
A cool, stone-walled, flag-floored room,
Full of old buckets, coils of twine, garden tools,
A washing basket at a still but crazy angle with a peg-bag in its lap,
And there is a huge fridge with a split handle,
Industriously buzzing in the heavy half-light.
A certain – knack – with the handle,
And the inside suddenly shows ranked remains of meals –
Today's, then yesterday's, behind those the day before's,
And then a whole pile of dishes, badly-bundled clingfilm packets,
A tubular clot of cooked chicken livers,
And saucers with bones on. Natural relics.
A cold smell of cabbage, peppermint, blood and cream arises from
    the shelves.
Hurry back in sunlight with the green herbs for tonight's meal.

Going Swimmingly

The blue-rinsed pool is full of rhythmic, lone strokers.
It drew us in from the edges as though it were blotter-dry and we
    were rushing liquid.
Swimming, an occasional, unseen toe contact
Seems to come long after the other solemn face bobbed by;
The body lengthens, a pale streamer drifting out under a Chinese
    lantern.

Standing in the pool, blinking and pinching your nose, brings
A strange slewed perspective down to the wavering floor –
Firm, cream shoulders, telescoped to no trunk,
Standing on skewing, marbled shimmypuppet legs,
Fatdappled with fallen blue petals of curling light.

Swimming, everything is simplified.
The eye level so low, a baby's out along the drunken carpet.
A rhythmic peace, of rocking and being rocked,
Plaiting yourself into the water,
Ploughing an intricate, soft turtle-track along the undersurface,
Each stroke a silver link in the chain that melts behind you.

Sheer weight and size of water!
Remembering some geography and its clean, cross-section
    diagrams –
The sea is an upside-down mountain of water,
An upturned yogi
Alive with pulling, fluid muscles;
A pressing city of water; a universe;
The town pool is an inverted block of flats, something
Gathered and gently milling. Container for a small revolution.

Hands trying to pray. Legs slowly trying to fly.
Simple, straining juxtapositions –
Waterbuffalo! Hovercraft! Starfish!
The water on fire in volcanoes and set in earth in amber!

The swimmer broaches a strange but yielding density;
Leans quietly into a huge, enfolding flank.
Reaches over, forward and out; to re-test the limits,
Smooth the limbs,
Of a rediscovered lover.

Goldeneye

This stone held heat long after its sun
     had rolled on: it waited.

This stone then cooled, its dome engaging in the socket of darkness.
     A rock almond, quietly gathering oil;

Uncurled one breath along the thin flank of evening: it stirred
     the dipping wing-tip of light in the sky.

This stone had word from old godheads. A demand for
     a cortex all skull, shaped slow by their hands alone;

But this stone hummed a growing note it would release
     when clapped open on the rock of truth: rehearsed

Its own unshelling. One and all. A freeze-dried seed of old light
     inverting to white downdrift of manna. Windfall.

Steeplejack

Entering the churchyard
I tread the stone steps' outer edge,
Hauling on the rail, to save their centres
Like an old wife with a new carpet.
On my back a heavy, soft clinking
Of oiled wooden handles and smooth iron,
Rolled and tied in warm leather;
I unsling the bag,
Place it clear of the white-flowered nettles.

Foxtail grasses crowd the graveyard wall,
Fidgeting in dusty sunlight.
Shafts of silver green, slow blend
Up through burgundy, to soft sandpuff of seeds.

A garden snail
Slides up a slim iris blade,
Feeling everything with its moist eye-tips,
Its shell a hardened whirlpool
Of concentration.

The job starts with
The moment of looking.
Send your eye up the spire
To hook to the top.
Lash your gaze to the weathercock's spurs
And unreel a rope back to the brain.
Assess the sides for footholds.
Take only tools you trust.
Leave the belfry shutters fastened back
When you start climbing
Straight up into the weather;
And then, when you come back,
It's easier. You're stepping in

From open light to dark —
The tricky part.

You only look the next inch up
Once each toe and finger and knee are wedged
Tight. Keep flat. Think flat, move one thought at a time.
Use your breathing like another limb.
Greet by private name each stone, each slate,
Each starblot of lichen,
Swept clean by rivers of air.

On windy days, the white air smashes round
Like a painting broken over you.
Your head's up through the back of the canvas;
Lookout in the ship of fools,
Skimmed by whirring swifts and swallows.

Never look around until the job is done.
Only wavered once in fifteen years of climbing;
A day of many weathers,
The wind in the hard north-east.
I'd just finished, spat out the last nail sideways,
Stowed away the hammer —
Then grasped the rope, and turned my face out, careful, to the land,
Slopes mixing green farms and bleakness . . .

And I thought, as slow as speaking,
All up from nowhere:
God — give this carpet — one good shake.
Let me leap up and out of it, for good.

The old man told me once on a bender
I was no better than a monkey,
Clinging to the spire like a mother's leg.
Thought of a picture I'd see in lessons of
Screaming monkeys, mad with fleas,
All pout and yellow peg-teeth and crashing branches.

Old sod was shouting, thin-lipped round a jerking fag-end,
Waving his skinny arms about.
Looked just like a chimp's twin brother.

I'm quiet as a rule, don't say much.
Sometimes disappear a while
Once or twice, on the year-end.
Found astride the lychgate singing hymns,
The heavy padlock swinging empty,
Picked open like a startled crab in my fist.

Girls talk to me. More than to the priest,
With his fishwhite face upturned, away from them,
His dead black dress.
They tell their feelings to the man
Who climbs to the eye of the ginger sun;
And steps back to earth each time for the love of it.

Sometimes when I'm working at
Crawling up God's nose,
I think of the wooden egg I'm carving for my wife.
It's best walnut, seasoned;
Smoky whorls like tumbling clouds
Or good meat laced through with fat.
Fresh egg, heavy in the hand. Rocket-clean as a kiss
While cupping the back of the other head.

Iken Cliff

The estuary lies like spilt milk on an open map;
A statement of fact, beautiful in its simplicity from the clifftop
As a good host bearing a wide, full platter in to a party;
Arresting in its detail to those who plash and slurp in the mud below,
Gazing into hollows and fingering the textures, like lovers.

A stout clinkerbuilt boat labours in the centre of the channel.
A boy stands up from the oars for a moment and laughs,
Calls up to one of the clifftop gardens,
Pretends to teeter over the boat's side,
Lobs an oath up for his friend to catch and enjoy.
His friend is swinging up there on an old tractor tyre, lashed to a tall
    dark fir tree.
He swings and swings, flashing like a cufflink,
Flying out and back at the enduring view,
Shooting his legs hard away over the distant church,
Full of a needed confidence that nothing will change –
Gripping hard; slows down to twizzle on the ropes in sudden
    forceful centrifuge
And enjoy the rise and flop of waves of sickness, hair flying.
Two laughters swoop out over water, then mingle in the air like
    smoke and steam.
One boys wears the splash of inspirational red that Constable
    always put artfully
Somewhere in his landscapes, alleviating the green or marine and
    grey.

The boat passes; now only walking figures slowly probe the skin of
    this scene,
Moving, faintly parasitic, down among the crisp froth of debris on
    the water's edge.
Sucking black and tan mud with a layer of crust like yoghurt,
Sediment of hundreds of Suffolk farms now nips at the heels.
Dogs roll and crash with joy here in their foul-smelling paradise,

Teeth etched white against the black and pink rivulets of sloppily-
    open mouth,
Sullied pennant tails up in a breeze crackling stiff with salt and fish.
A damp mosaic of crabshells, tarry sticks and caviar ooze
Laid out around them, their own huge open picnic field.

These clinking grey pebbles are a million fossil eggs
Held up to the sky for inspection in this tortoiseshell mudbowl.
Walking on eggshells.

All the estuary is still there, canvas-cool,
And yet compelling; oddly flat as a mirage,
Like the junior artist's tussle with perspective,
With the rug that won't lie down.
In a space as wide as vision, there is a need for focus, detail,
Either fingered and felt on bone, or recorded in the eye;
A need to pick and to possess one thing;
The stone shaped like a tiny owl turning its head right around,
The serious boy carrying the picnic glass of wine to his father, using
    both hands.

Plumbline

This body of loved music leans close in, to breathe directly in your
　　nostrils;
A bullish mass, viewed from below, underlines the summer sky.
It unclasps a fluid pouch of a bass line;
A soft kick in the pocket;
Idling yet full
Bass line, ploughing the loam of the smaller self;
Spreading it, like knees.
The boom swings deep across the boat towards you,
The tinkling curtain parts and up it comes, the
Lowing bass line, head to the rolling ground,
A tiger's cough, disarming:
Not which way to run, but whether, to this
Push and pull of sound from the ring of surrounding hills.

Thick turning cable, taproot and sinew of sound;
Young hooves pestling on old mud,
One warm thunder without threat,
The beat and the note loping together in three dimensions,
Screwing right down to a never-sticking point.
And the soft-shell underparts of the music, not bone nor flesh,
Endlessly sailing up from dark to light;
Rhythm of the hung moment,
Gathering on the swung edge of the outer arc,
　　　　breasting the rim between forward and plummet . . .
Somewhere an armadillo rolls over and smiles at the sun.

The first time I felt like this I was a small child
Making butter curls in a summer room,
Skimming the meek shining ingot in its white dish;
Judging the amount just right,
Counting the warm oily waves, ribbed in gold.
A soft cairn of butter for chosen guests, who would offer
Curls of richness to one another on the miniature knife,

Its worn horn handle, yet blunt-bladed innocence;
The rich mineral bite of parsley.
I hadn't yet seen John Belushi's eyebrows,
But maybe if I had, I'd've understood.

And back slides the music, round to the probing nub;
That funneling bass line, fluxing dark,
Centripetal suction nudging the notes out and back,
Warm waves that lift the feet from the sandbank,
And place them exactly one firm foot away – deft implantation;
No consonants, no cormorants in this sea of folding inflections,
Alluvial sound and sunk bullion; moody slippage,
Confluent domes, warm running spine of woven ovals.
Come, soft-bucking sea, we crave a boon, a boon.

Cuckoo-spit

Cuckoo-spit on cowparsley.
The snowfroth parts under the finger, and inside
Sits the wicked-looking wet froglet of bilious bright green,
Quiet in his homespun castle,
Waiting.

The child screams, spins round, flip-wipes her hand
On thigh in one flamenco movement;
Then returns, and looks again.

Beach Scene with Small Figure

For Guy

Walking the easy, open beach,
Through the coastline's gappy, disarming smile,
Turning on the currents of an idling mind,
Slow human flotsam, no hurry;
This gently curving walk
Brings back the Yorkshire terrierhood of the small child;
The short sticklegs, gleaming white parting,
Thin hair pulled up into rubberbands,
Quick-eyed, probing into cracks in the prone reptile of the rock,
Testing everything.
Every smell on the beach is savoury, astringent.

Raise a stone with a long seawide seaweed ribbon,
An old chariot track made vegetable,
Hold it up shining rich phlegm colour in the clear light,
The single terrible suction foot
Clamped in black to the salt-licked stone.
Here comes the snaking fear
That the wind will swoop in,
Flap and curl the wet ribbon about bare legs,
A cold hand slapping,
And nowhere to jump to.

Striated sands. Many pools resting, curled in sleep
While channelling the sky.

Walk on, up the splayed wind, to the single point.

Combustion Engine

*'The combustion engine is built on the principle
of a series of controlled explosions'*

The street-traders were roaring and steaming,
Stuffing loose bananas rudely into bags,
Unpouching greasy pennies. Dogs stared,
Tomatoes rolled from boxes, and the busy roadside
Receded at once to a frieze
Intricate but still as a chain of paper dolls,
When the low-slung motorbike passed by;
Its spun-out note blown flat but steady.

Slow bullet, low throttle,
Loud with smoke and choke and oil;
Its combustion just contained
In the two raised fists of a silver, black and blue
Bearded rider. Dark-shaded eye of this smoky storm,
Cruising on the base of his spine,
Bootsoles, metal toecaps and lean, wide crotch first, advancing . . .

The small girl takes one step aside a moment
Under the peck and bob of her mother's basket.
She stands neatly, small socks level, feet together on the kerb,
One hand pressed under her collar, on the dry pucker of smocking –
And flips one quick, instinctive wave at him –
Matter-of-factly, just fingers moving. The biker passes,
Head of an invisible procession. Trawler of eyes,
Careless fisher of widening looks,
His backwash unfurls along the street.

Answers on a Postcard

A wave of migrating beasts
Pummels hard and wide,
A single-minded storm on the drumtight earth.
No husbanding of strength for the long future,
But open-handed spending of energy ablaze.
A ship's boiler, stoked full and smoking, breaks loose —
Rolls over the curved and smoothly cruising deck,
Wrestling in its skin like grown brothers' thoughts of each other.

Unseen until their presence marked it,
The creatures' track is known by mind's eye alone.
Not a trail with beginning and end,
But always as one point, right now,
To be rolled back, away, on the earthball beneath the feet.
That point then sparks ahead from star to star,
Its spoor blunt-snouted directly by heart and feet;
Impelling first to run, then dissolve, and boil along it.
Each animal a gasping red-eyed sack, drunk on instinct,
Slung over a set of four legs that, rocking, run and run and run
To press the ancient, desert rock-hard, burning forehead against
    that soft horizon,
Smooth and cool as a saint's ascending foot.

This unruliness has other ends.
It pricks out design; a web too great
For relevance to the spinning inhabitant.
What is done from within, only others can clearly see.
Migration cannot think, it does not care which end is home.

Up the Brook

The stream in its clay bed
Ran a single knot-hole right through the brown village;
Opening out of farmland far up country
Past the badgers under the thornbushes,
Then sliding down as far as the town, maybe further:
The coast, with its annual level horizon,
Distant as the rings of a planet.

Retracing smaller steps up the brook
Using the may-trees as pulling bones
To get you up and over the water in one swing;

A dam to be built, first with a roughly settled brick,
Then friable crusts of sandstone, dark gold
And smudgy in the hands as Egyptian eyeliner,
Pegged one by one in the blubber of mud,
A shallow twirling between the stones;
Party jelly through teeth.
Mud floats open like nylon stockings into the water,
The uncoiling heads of ferns.

Deep sheep hoofprints make simple oily pools in the starred mud,
Reflecting twin uncertain eyelets of sky.
Brown soup-pools of slow-turning bubbles and floating pods.
Long games with bits of stick and dirt,
Dock leaves and nettles, shrimps shrugging along.
An old labrador is called back; two notes overarching –
Lifted bodily over the deep bits,
Blurting short-legged through thick mud.
A toehold on the wall and into a place hard to speak of,
Instead of named village lanes
And places with edges, owners.

On a boat, the *Sea Cow*, in North Norfolk,
I was once allowed to touch
A collection of white stones and bones
In a tiny, doll-like porthole;
Felt a pliant sack of huge thrills
At being the only sets of footprints on this island;
At running with another old dog, this one black,
Taking possession by the nose of the beach and dunes.

Winter in August

Winter once came so early, it approached in high summer
While all the world was away on picnics.

A wanted child,
Tadpoled into a potbound monster,
Wore the thin house to bursting,
Rode it nearly to death.
Too big now to cry for old pets, for stopped comics;
Too small for the evening youth club, the motorbikes,
Right size for nowhere but the corner, on the carpet
With the scuffed and splitting box of records.

Bear out this droughty, silent winter.
And who to appeal to, for something you can't describe?
Something so urgent it's not thought of directly —
Tapping, worming; resilient, moist,
Gaggier than warm bacon rind
That pushes and coils in greasy white question marks
Around the rim of the plate, insistent.
The child swings, bored,
On the back door, one foot in the catflap,
Banging shut and springing open,
Droning under the breath.

Now let us pray:
Oh God, send invitations.
Parties. Then stay at their house.
Just normal.

The Minotaur

The head, held low, is heavier than a blunt shovel in clay
As the creature pans the slow-circling dark for smells.
He stands in the earth,
A crop of animal heat and steam among stones,
Something slowly come to a head.
The dark centre of gravity in that massed body
Is the nowhere of everywhere at once.
Traffic in the web of a steady city whirls in one dimension,
Showing no centre, nor target, but one low sustained note
Strung consistent from limb to limb, beaten in the panels of the
    skull.

Without a fulcrum, there is no neat counterpoint, no play;
Maybe, with luck, a short life as tool to a greater force.
The single fact of a shot put,
One close-fisted thump, squat full stop in damp sand,
Not poised but simply there, no skip or roll.

He breathes with the stolid suction and release of a sleeper.
Dark processes skate under his skin,
Quietly accreting bone on bone.

He has stood in this spot for the slow blink, for the leapt year of a
    coma.
Solitary time, and an animal's time,
Have no measure except empty and full.
Loosely gazing, unfocused,
He licks salt from the fault-line cloven in the rock.
Its jagged line sears in from where a sky used to beam
Clear as a god's conscience,
Then forks; two spurs drive down
Through the ground and into the stone chamber,
The straw leaching with rottenness.

Passageways gape in the dark around him, fanned out
In the even chaos of dropped and splintered glass.
The shape of shock smashed out on the floor
And just left to lie there. A frozen whirlwind.

The many-chambered heart of the labyrinth hangs low between his
 horns;
Its matrix somehow sick,
  something pulsing too slow, too slow quite to come to
   consciousness;
A dry teat. Space ever latent.

————————

A long slow scratch on the long low lintel,
A dream of a scratch,
Leaning into the fatty line of hair on the stone's lip.
Blocks of stone so sandy pale they look soft,
Great blunt cubes, with tracery of glitter and pink net:
I dream – or remember? – lapping at
Honey droplets anointing a wide pat of halva;
Powdery, pliant loukoum, the oily velvet crunch of pistachio nut.

Pale flames of fern cluster along the stains on the walls
Like starving figures waving at a roadside.
I coil them in with my tongue and drink their chill in turn,
And now I want meat. The hot sweetness of meat.
Roast, scorched even, steaming blasphemy of blood.
Cracked wheat crust. Tart mustard.

I sometimes wake too suddenly, before I can re-invent myself,
And hear the midwife's cries stuffed back behind both hands,
A mad bird stuck and beating in a chimney.
My head-bones, still soft under pressure
Knit the cries into the skull as it set.
I lay heaped, a doll thrown in a corner,
And yearned for licking to assemble me into life,
The comfortable work of a spatulate tongue to articulate me,

Define my spine and quietly
Gather in the jerky dropped bundle of legs.
I lay untouched, and then slowly introduced myself,
First to myself,
Reeling in,
Trying to hold a thought against the screaming.

Later on, twin sticky-buds of new pain grew
Insistent on my head, needing their sore velvet to be rubbed and
    rubbed away
On the rolling tip of my shoulder, always just out of reach.

My own heart has thickened by the weight of earth all around,
Beats too bulky for these ribs. But here it is quiet, this stone bowl
A holding-place for thought. Before this place
I moved from cries of pain behind into cries of fear ahead,
A stony pilgrimage for someone else's penance
Who gave birth wearing a mask for the shame of it all.

The teams of sweating labourers on this pit were brought down
    from the hills,
Fiddling with their clasp-knives, their moneybags,
Working fast over my head to block out the light.
They worked that day as roofers on solid ground,
But still dared not look down.
Stones thudded onto beams, scarring one another's faces,
Then earth was scraped in with the shoulder-blades of oxen
And the job was done by early evening.
They rushed for the hills, troll-like,
Used to dealing in darkness.

Light footsteps circle overhead.
A young boy dances, practising his vaulting, partnering the sun.
On one side of this bear-pit an old and flaking frieze in red
Shows those lambent boys, the naked dancers with the bulls,
Tumbling like minnows in bright water around a single black rock.
They use the bull's lowered face as a blunt mounting block,

The skull as stepping stone, from his moment of confusion
Up and out, into the watchers' halo of shining eyes –
Women, admirers, loving the bruising of a serpent's head.
Hollowed stone bowls are brought to catch the beast's blood.
It is mixed with ochre for the priestess, creatrix;
Warm paint – still darkening – for her body.

Priestess and dungbeetle, both find their function.
I am the black fruit of the life of this city,
Held on a bad stem between sky and earth,
Not yet full, or sick, enough to drop.
What I am for, I cannot see. I cannot help myself.

The Dreaming Bean

This is the germinal spot of gathering green.
A close-curled, blissful fist
Of dreaming bean, milk-wet opal in the pod.

Held in the damp, white hollow of down,
The touch of light sifts through slim walls of sap
Circling, drifting cool and fine, to a whispertip.

A juicebubble; single, wetblown membrane,
Sphere of spun water, held high to the sun
In convergent slipstreams of light and air.

Not yet a thing of earth, the bean lies curled and
Swelling into itself, welling like a favourite thought.
Its stem is a pointing finger, to focus colour, meaning and delight.

The stem refines, and then instils a greater world;
A gathering up and soundless pouring into a quiet green pool.
A flow of growing vision into the beholding eye.

The pod moves – small wimple, turning on the breeze –
And steadies again. The dreaming bean
Makes the slightest of slipping squeaks against the skin
Like a wet finger on the boat's white hull.

A drop of breathing seasound in the sappy shell,
Starting to dream of changing state,
Of firming the sap to smoothness,
Of forming two soft, mirrorlinked halves;
This bean, the young old milk-tooth of the earth.

Swim Right Up to Me

I first learnt to swim at home in my father's study
On the piano-stool, planted on the middle of the rug.
Stomach down, head up, arms and legs rowing hard;
I swam bravely, ploughing up the small room,
Pinned on a crushed stuckness of stomach to tapestry,
The twin handles hard on my elbows on the back-stroke.
A view down through four braced wooden legs
To the same thin spot in the rug.
My mother faced me, calling rhythmic encouragement,
Almost stepping back to let me swim up to her,
Reminding me to breathe;
And wiping my hair and eyes with her hand
As I swam and swam on the furniture against a running tide,
Pig-cheeked, concentrating on pushing and pushing away,
Planning to learn to fly next, easy,
Higher than the kitchen table, even. The garden wall.

Mrs Salmon

Planted, unsmiling, for required photograph
Stands the white-haired figure of a woman, shoulders back.
She gazes for all the future from the black box of now,
With the level simplicity of an animal.

This is Mrs Salmon.

She wears her clothes firmly.
She likes them to move in formation
Exactly when and where she does. No floating around.
A fierce, fun-nautical, tightly packed and buttoned blazer
Brim-full of a single horizontal line of breast,
The fabric hard to the eyes' touch.
The crisp hat an exact match, its narrow brim
A line of guttering rimming the village church.
Utterly fire-retardant, inside and out.

Her deep eyes know something that will never be referred to.
Your blood searches, childlike,
For any link with her, where there is none.
It finds instead the leader of a grim but just tribe,
With one clear demand for its fixed tithe –
Acknowledgement.
It finds a being incarnated from the badger
Who dug, brave because he had to be,
Right through the waiting line of terriers.

Horse-doctor

Little old man with a strong farmyard smell on him
Of mud and damp rubber and root vegetables
Totters into this yard, bandy as a baby,
And can tell straight off what's wrong with a pony
Just from being quiet in the stable with it a while.
Sees things in the way they use their eyes,
Gets ideas or hunches suddenly, same as they do;
Or standing in the paddock, watches which herbs they pull
From far back in the hedgerow.
Sees which way their need will drive them.

Can tell if there's a speck of mould in the hay.
Gets out an old curry-comb with half the teeth gone,
Then runs it through the coat and smells
With his head down and mouth open at it like a dog.
He drenches a sick one using an old horn,
And a blue glass bottle with a crusty cork.
They'll take it. They'll be kicking the place down,
Flaring, all teeth and eyes and flattened ears,
Then go all quiet under his hands,
While we can't get behind them, can't get near them.

The dogs love him. He brings a bag of bits for them;
Best of all when he's seen the blacksmith for the parings.
Throws them crescent moons of hoofcuts –
A rind still burnt and smoky
That goes pattering down on the stones – the dogs rushing for them.
Could be anything in that blue glass bottle,
But the old feller knows his stuff all right.
He'll part a pile of droppings with his boot and
Show you the story in it – can tell the weather from it –
Like those Eskimos with all their snow,
Twenty different kinds of shit, at least.

Invalid Days

A file of invalid days slips past the still bed,
A grey string dragged to tempt a bored cat.
This bodyload, this tilting wheelbarrow,
Will not become bearable.
Everything must simply wait,
As polite but brisk walkers for stragglers at a stile.

Into the bare facts of the invalid's existence
Comes the blunted twinkle of a guitar, strummed next door.
It tells, though filtered, of comfort
In close lives. Other lives.

Their music grates. They can't sing.
It's hateful to hear their enjoyment.

Sit still! Smaller than still! The pain is returning;
The hurt rolls its glowing boulder, gathers force,
Rears up from the molten bowels of the earth –
Huge and heavy, streaming with the pollen of change –
About to write a terrible word,
Squeaking on the thin slate of the body.

Save me. Let it pass.

It passes. At the high edge of the bedroom, or of the larger world,
A slight, dark movement tugs the ropes of the drifting eye;
The whisking of a thought perhaps, that took the curve of time for
    space.
Certain images can still cock the sleeping mind;
Migrated thoughts long outspun, long hulled.
The old dog on his chain stiffly barks at night-blown papers.

The irregular effervescence of a night breeze prickles the poplar
    leaves.
Long pauses between noticings, a detachment.
The steady daylong flow of the river

Remembered by one passing knot of driftwood.
Like a collector of frail china,
The invalid handles the world one slim segment at a time.

Activity is suspended. The invalid withdraws,
Cancelled out. And finds the chaos is all within.
Holding it there in its blind pink squirming like a kitten under water
   whose breath will not finish and will not finish
Takes all,
All the long time and small energy in his world.
The angels dance singly on the point of his needle.
He feels each of their million burning feet.

Cats Are Otherwise

Cat steps into the house; courteous,
But still privately electrified by the garden. His fur,
Plump with light as the breastfeathers of the young god of air,
Implies brush-bruised geraniums, and herbs:
Fruitmusk webs of blackcurrant groves
Rusting slowly in an old sun:
A slow-unrolling afternoon
Asleep on the warm earth, above fresh bird-bones.

Cats know control as the basis of magic.
They are our slimmer selves,
That peel doors open to slip out – all eyes – and are gone;
May or may not report back
The easy cruelties of the perfectly adapted, the over-civilized.

When they yawn, a hot zigzag rose blown deep open
Amazes with its pinkness.
The yawn seems bigger than their whole head, like a snake's.
Two eyes slip, soft yolks on a bone brink, right back into their ears.

Cats may not care to offer up each thought. We look on them;
And remain, like children on the stairs at a dinner party,
Acknowledged by that other world,
Yet uninvited; and so not fully present.

Dogs Just Are

A large dog is husk for the soul of an Ancient Briton,
Already wild, and now just discovered poteen. Roughly distilled.
He prefers the rounding-up of others as his own definition.

Dogs live entirely in the here and now. Head-on.
Questions not immediately answered are instantly let go.
They have the perfect sincerity of the fanatic.

Dogs have fun; for they inhabit
The centre of a cartoon world, a brilliant sketch of extremes;
Bone idle, or bursting with intent on passwords, gangs, explosive
    games;

The thrilling squirm of total noise. Pure shouting. It defies, defeats
    the world:
Short-circuits the brain, pressed hard out from the stomach,
Eyes shut, chest down, throat wide, earbones ringing like a tin tray
    on concrete.

Drumming and yelling, dog tribes retreat and advance on the
    common,
Heavy in skunky, tasselled fleeces, treadmilling along,
Great tough old waterbirds who flog a river surface,
Trying to run right up the sky.

Diving Board

Brand-new girlish breaststroke up and down the town pool,
A cool pearl button through silk-frogged buttonholes,
An elision fluid and oval as a French vowel;
You are proud of your chlorinated otterings.
A haze of talc, wet hair and hot Bovril from tiered orange seats
Floats bellyup to a streaming glass ceiling abuzz with neon.

The tough oilsleek diving board stands dark as a pithead crane,
A pointing steel gundog straining for the falling star.
Room for another flea on its back.
A long black tongue is ready for your feet.

Leg-up the ladder onto the board? – Dare you to.
Warty and tense underfoot,
It's like walking out along a great toothless gumline.
With small, rude leaks and poppings from your bathing suit,
You're a kipper gone cold in its cleaving bag.

This is a rock-face swaying in a high wind.
A concrete trampoline.
Judge it wrong, and you break your jaw on the toffeehammering end,
Or burst like a fig, swooping from the kindly tree onto tarmac.

Walk back to the safe end, firm on its silver rollers.
Just let the loud boys go through first.

Go.

A dull spong and a few metallic knockings, like a dying engine
Flip you up and over.
Sweet as a perfectly-served tennis ball;
Murderous, invisibly aflame with topspin.
Then a pebbledashed implosion,
Shrugging down like a dynamited building
In the suddenly spanked and yelling water.

Bird at the Window

Smashed down here,
On crushed balsa-wood wings
Flayed to matchsticks.
Crashed down here on the path,
Pegged out on shock's nails
As if under glass for a connoisseur.

Self not sure if face down or up –
Too late to care;
Legs and wings and beak stubbed out,
Thrown far around. The shock of spirit to matter.
Wet exclamation of a dropped egg –

Flew piping, then slammed and fell
Hard down through sudden flatness –
Fell broadsides and straight through:
Left a you-sized hole in the sky,
Small beads of your self
Still skirling away on impact,
The soft kink of death in the neck,
White eyelids rising.

Above you in the concentration of thick glass
Hangs my face,
Caught in your envisioned tree, still rippling.

Intent

Two check rugs and a straw mat on the ground,
Hot as a living bone.
The odd lizard flickers past and stops a moment.
Its mouth is shut but its whole attitude seems gaping,
Listening, fingers spread flat up the wall like an eavesdropper.

Only a few days camping, and
Even the young grass looks stained and rumpled.

A camp-stove tilts smoking water to a choky boil.
The car-key, popped out of its broken plastic pincher,
Is pressed sharp down in the earth inside the tent flap
In case of thieves, who might want all this.

Two people on holiday in silence,
Neither of whom seem to have a name;
Like the lizard, a species in themselves,
Unspecified.

Him, listening to sports results on the car radio,
Thighs spread easy on the front seat,
Spitting grape pips out of the window.

Her, slow with heat on the rug,
Re-arranging small picnic things,
Brooding. Occupying life from the inside.

This Dead Relationship

I carry a dead relationship around everywhere with me.
It's my hobby.
How lucky to have a job that's also my hobby,
To do it all the time.

A few people notice, and ask if they can help carry this thing.
But, like an alcoholic scared they will hear the clink of glass in the bag,
I refuse – scared they'll smell rottenness,
Scared of something under their touch
That will cave in, a skin over brown foam on a bad apple.
I cram this thing over the threshold
Into the cold and speechless house,
Lean against the front door for a moment to breathe in the dark,
Then start the slow haul to the kitchen.
Steek knives catch the moonlight on white tiles.

This dead relationship.

Or not yet dead.

Or dead and half-eaten,
One eye and one flank open, like a sheep under a hedge.

Or dead but still farting like the bodies in the trenches,
Exploding with their own gas. Hair and nails still growing.

It has the pins and needles of returning feeling in a deadness.
It is a reptile in my hand, quick and small and cool;
The flip of life in a dry, cold bag of loose skin.
A pressure without warmth of small claws and horn moving on my palm.

At night it slips slow but purposeful across the floor towards the bed.
Next thing it's looking out of my eyes in the morning –
And in the mirror, though my eyes are not my own,
My mouth shows surprise that I am still there at all.

Oh, a sickness that can make you so ill,
Yet doesn't have the decency to kill you.
A mad free-fall that never hits the ground,
Never knows even the relief of sudden shock;
Just endless medium-rare shock, half-firm, half-bloody all the time.
A long, slow learning curve.
The overheating that can strip an engine badly,
Strain it far worse than a racing rally.
The fear that you will slow to a stop
Then start a soft, thick, slow-gathering roll backwards.

I want something that is familiar but not.
To feel in someone else's pocket for a key
While they lean away, laughing, their arms up,
Hands in the air covered in grease or dough or paint or clay.

I have to carry it around.
A weeping mother brings a baby to hospital,
Late-night emergency.
The tired doctor smooths the hand-made lace back from its face.
He sees it was stillborn weeks ago, has been dead for weeks.
He looks at her, there is no air in the room . . .

This dead relationship. This dead and sinking ship.
Bulbs lie, unplanted, on a plate of dust.
Dry and puckered pouches, only slightly mouldy;
Embalmed little stomachs but with hairy, twisted fingers,
Waiting for something to happen without needing to know what it is.
When it happens everything else in the universe can start.

This dead relationship.

I am this thing's twin.
One of us is dead
And we don't know which, we are so close.

Saltmarsh and Skylark

A man sits in a bowl of sunlight on the saltmarsh, clearly alone.
A slight hollow brings shelter on this husky threshing floor,
Stamped out flat by heavy, working weather.

The marshes are etched by veins of water so salt
It rustles faintly as it flows; sequin platelets buffed bright by acid –
So salt it iceburns, with the stick and pull of skin on frosted metal.

The water is carding its knotty white strings slowly
Through the blue brown fish-flesh of the mud.
Slowly laces and unlaces the filaments in the corridor of gills.

The marsh is a scribble of tough whip-grass and matted vetch;
Cross-hatched collage of God's leftovers;
Odd peelings from the plughole, pilled tweed
And steel wool, glued on in tufts by a nervous understudy.

Dry brown curves of grass, bowing down in pools of white light;
A crumbling-rusk-in-skimmed-milk landscape.
The man squints upwards into larksong and closes his eyes.

As he tilts, he inhales the song all the warm way up the light.
The eyelids thinly filter, impressing into hot blood-orange,
Then melting crabshell, embossed in pink and greening bronze;

Strange bunching and wellings, expansive dissolution;
The matt black stamen of the skylark's turning tongue,
The brain-stem's softly-bound bouquet of pulses.

Fenland Station in Winter

The railway station in winter lies wide open on three sides;
A waiting mousetrap.
No creatures out in the hard fields,
The desert of blue-lipped ice.
The tracks tweeze the last thin train away,
Wipe it on the rim, and lose it.

The sky is bent so low now, the wind is horizontal.
It whittles the sky's undersurface to the pith,
Paring away a grey unwinding peel of snow.
A mean, needling flake rides the flat wind,
Picking the empty teeth of the trees,
Then falling, frantic, to gnaw at the setting earth,
Clinging there like a starving mouse's claws in velvet.

Not Yet in Season

Two new friends walk, unmerged,
Through thin woods not yet alive to spring;
Pale bones of scrubland
In an early Easter eggyolk sunlight.
The earth a stretch of placid pastry
Waiting for transforming warmth
To give it shape and risen smell, and meaning.

In the darkening paddock, flea-dirt dotted with hopping crows,
Spinach-oily ponypats pool the last of the evening light.
The low hawthorns are combed hard back,
All pointing inland
To where the wind went.

Back in the cool cottage, the fire is wavering,
Clutching at straws, nearly out.
'We can save it if we act this minute.'
With the politeness of the newly-known
(Over-attentive to animal matters, preparing food and warmth
But nobody mentioning bed yet),
Each spends several minutes pretending they don't mind
Being the one to fetch the damp logs,
Wimmelling alive with woodlice, from the rented shed.
They walk there together, silent, through the chattering dark.

Dr Emmet's Chairlegs

The study was full. Papers sloughed
Their yellow scales in deep drifts on the little floor.
So he bent carefully from the knees, and somehow from the arms,
And slowly piled two chairs on one another;
Top one upside down, its tacks showing;
Shoulders on the floor, frozen mid-jive,
As in summer-holiday classrooms or emptying bars.

He stacked papers in the upturned lap-legs of the top chair.
Fixed them in space by patting them twice,
Absently. Maritally. Would know just where to go,
If this research were ever needed.
Old pilots know by touch even the dried and rootless riverbeds.

Doing this gave the satisfaction
Of opening a door onto the night,
And dropping a bag in the dustbin –
That momentary lessening of weight upon the frame;
The instinct afterwards to straighten up,
Rub the hands and look briefly around,
Check the weather and the stars, before moving on,
A small pleasure riding the in-breath.

McGregor Road

Children fight loudly on the pavement in a tight, happy clot.
A small princess emerges above them,
Treads slowly down her front steps,
A gold cardboard crown on her kid's slippery straight hair,
A string of squashed tissue flowers wound over a woolly cardigan
Buttoned up all wrong, splayed over a bunchy summer dress.
Her sister leads her down to the pavement.
The sister is bigger, in mother's black stilettos.
A metallic pock then a rending dry steel howl
As she half-steps, half-shuffles, dragging the tall heels
In a swarm of sound like falling scaffolding.
She skis inside the shoes, crouched high on a crazy angle,
Skewering the weeds between flagstones.

They stand and watch together gravely, absorbed,
Chewing with their mouths open.

The others are busy bashing a loose old skateboard,
Cheerfully, consciously cruel to the smaller ones,
Playing in short bursts of intensely casual violence.

High walls throw back the spiralling yells
As they place a wide plank across the skateboard,
And sit the smallest boy on it for a wild ride
Which he loves, clinging to the splintering sides and screaming
As the plank swivels and smacks the thin town trees.

The princess is wearing soft slippers
With Mickey Mouse faces on the fronts.
'Pig!' she shouts in general, spinning, aiming a kick at the air.

Osmosis

The water is to swimmer as a kiss
Placed on a closed but moving eye.
And swimmer is to water
As a ghost to a claiming room.
The swimmer – suspended, flickering –
Parts the soft walls in the thickened realm
Of an element not entirely owned;
A bladder of heavy air,
Embodied; and yet boneless.

Jesus in Totnes

I saw Jesus in Totnes. Twice.
I knew it was him, because at five I knew a lot.
I'd been to Sunday school, and even won a small prize
For the neatest drawing of God (no rubbing-out).
Although there had been setbacks too.
When teacher asked what mankind was descended from,
I'd answered first, in total assurance:
'Sheep.' All the village kids
Hooted loud; they knew they were apes.
I'd believed in the Good Shepherd, with us as his flock,
The flowing robes, the crook and the hawthorns.
Not in a big ape.
I ran away so fast the tears shot horizontal in my hair.
Sat raging in the shrubbery for an hour.

Devon was big sheep-farming country
And there, walking down the high street, was Christ
In clean white cheesecloth and strings of love-beads.
Everything in me rushed out to greet him, while the street stood still.

Later in the post-office, fisting stamps onto postcards,
I saw him again; and quietly stood behind him,
Smelt the hem of his salty shirt.
There was a long bronze woman with him, in cut-off denims.
Jesus's hand moved across at thigh-level – my eye-level –
And squeezed the little earth-gold crescent of bottom peeking from
    her shorts.
I watched, from the peaceful almond eye of the storm of
    confirmation.

Sleeper

He falls asleep.
Helps himself to a scoop of sleep,
One hand up to the face, quite simply,
Like a fat man at the peanuts at a party;
Naturally. There to be taken.

The sleeper lies removed, smoothly replete;
Easy into it as a puppy's roll, one shoulder down,
Loose-headed, away over unseen contours.
Will wake with a swept mind.

The curtains swell in the night breeze just as
Thin peelrings turn softly, unwinding from the fruit.
Nights are the breaths in an idiot's anecdote,
Forgotten opening of doors between remembered rooms.

Pickle Jar

He slides out at lunchtime, catching a hip on the same old bruise;
Cannot look at the grey varicose of spaghetti
Skidding onto thick canteen china.
He walks to the patchy park, alone,
With the air both limp and hostile
Perfected by the British. Blindly picks pebbles
To lob at the dog-turd in the open smile of the sandpit.

The familiar arguments tumble to and fro in the brainbag.
Some old rocks never turn smooth —
Not with a lifetime of seastroke.
Thoughts scuff like kids' shoes,
Beating on the back of his eyeballs.

That night, a dry dream clatters on the bed's scree of stones;
A small nub of brain, pale in a pickle jar,
Shrunk as last winter's walnut;
Pushed to and fro by hands in argument —
Dragged across the lab's scarred bench,
A storm of bitter sediment obscuring the glassy view.

Vomit, Mind

Vomit, mind. And give up explaining.
Prise up the too-tight lid. An urgent
Slap-up soft-boiled vomit, spinning
Half up the walls, shambling back down in dying foam.
Retreating into cooling chaos.

Empty again, the mind is cudless,
Caved in, must sleep. Then
Information's regular rape can start the day.
New days are now not where you live,
But where you earn a living.

Vomit, mind. I'll watch the crash,
Impartial; a stranger at a party, a bad landing
Slammed on the hall rug in all your jewellery,
Face down, your boots half-on,
Maggot-grains of rice stuck soft between the floorboards.

And vomit office days, stacked up in A4 piles.
Spent. Dry eyes swiping a livid computer screen.
Bitten bones of days left stuck and cooling in the diary.
A red nib nosing the page, sniffing out failings,
Cocked for misdeeds. The punishment of tiny, fiddling marks.
Days as regular as the rasp of tin shovel on dry tarmac
Striking thin, blue, icy sparks.

Jake the Blind Dog

Jake the blind dog's lived
For his own forever in this farmhouse.
He creeps across the kitchen floor on the diagonal,
Reeling himself in along a dotted line of voices,
His blank eyes useless, over-bright
But still trained on the sound of his people.
He moves one leg at a time like a puppet dog, concentrating,
Getting mixed up in the rungs of chairs,
To stand in front of the open fridge
Side by side with the woman,
Both framed in its indifferent, pearly yawn;
Both smelling thoughtfully, considering different menus.
Steady ox and ass, unpuzzled at their radiant manger,
She gazing in, Jake dimly aware of light and
Not gazing, but thinking of gazing,
Down the twisted skein of smell to the bowl at the source.
Standing stiffly upright, peg-legs under thin shoulders,
He listens, content to be held there in the voice.
His balls are the last two nutmegs on a winter tree,
Wooden mushrooms turned in the heel of a thin black sock.
She – not bending, exactly – but roundly inclined forward
Largely from the hip, a soft-boiled egg aslant in the cup;
Talking to him, serving as his eyes and language,
Arms out over him
In the wide curve of hovering, skating, blessing,
Right hand up on the fridge door, left hand resting on the top.
Their figures linked in a dream of food;
Ringed wooden posts, held by the soft swag of the hammock.

Pardon

Dusk falls early in this lowering building,
Slipping between the thin-skinned prayer-books.

With only a slight squeaking of pedals,
The organist practises, flung grapeshot of red and gold blare;
Giving the sudden warning trills and rampant booms
Of a curious whale, soaring up out of darkness,
Banking neatly at the surface, examining Jonah out loud.
Blunt as the unconscious, about to remember.

One dim face gazes up at the gristly whaleboned ribbing
And waits inside the greyness of this beast
In soft but growing urgency, like an impending belch,
For the prophet – who, swallowed, must crash in above the altar,
Skidding down in skeltering tubfuls
Of gulped plankton in green water, arms up,
Shouting, prawns struggling in his beard –
Then the waiting palls.

People stir the shadowed edges of this space.
Hushed forms, idly scavenging without real hunger
For a role, dully opening and shutting their bags,
Observing the bones of architecture with ritual remarks,
Cockling for detail.
No interesting maggots in this carcass.
The painted-on angels doze in the high half-light,
Their lilies slipping slowly from their laps,
Nobody minding;
Everywhere the elderly tolerance of reduction
That creeps in unremarked, like rising dust,
And is in itself the greatest reduction.
The organist does steady scales to warm his hands,
Then shuts the book. Abruptly sneezes out the spores.

A Duck for God

The Chinese restaurant is the tiny front room
Of what was once a family town-house,
Now seeming to lean forward, so intent on its inner process
Of making exotic lunch –
Its honey, pan-clattering, smoke and fat, strange grasses, pods,
Curling un-named things in fragrant steam
Delivered from a muffled, yelling kitchen,
Glimpsed through a slamming hatch.

The window was once a porthole from a dim town sitting-room,
Bringing brief visions of the neighbours,
Who did and who did not wear gloves;
Now it's crisply filled with splayed red racks of spatchcocked fowl,
Notices of the daily specials, Visa signs, reviews from local papers;
A hot-mouthed coquetry for sharp passing hungers.

The window table is half-filled by one dark man
Alone; a large black telephone propped on the chopstick rest.
He sits still while eating fast from the small bowls,
Seeming to eat more with his hands than with his mouth;
Busy-eyed, watching his huge car crouch outside.
Another table stings with brief argument about office behaviours.

The Chinese waitress, slim as a licking tongue
In her boy's black trousers and waistcoat,
Climbs unremarked, cat's-eye quick, onto the back table:
Reaches tree-high to a painted shelf
A foot from a ceiling dim with oven-breath –
And slips her icon of a smiling god
The largest roast duck, basted crisp and perfect orange;
Pours him a thick, sweet drink up there in the high dark,
Pricks a velvet-headed joss-stick in the duck's fat honey-weeping
    thigh,
And slowly lights it, holding the god's steady golden gaze.

The Lie of the Land

Here on the high edge of the cliff
Only the breeze is moving under the spring sun.
When the breeze drops, insects vie loudly for the new space.

Footpaths cut a mild scar through scrub and gorse,
Following a course as a trickle of water would
Down the upturned face of the dunes, from the cliff
To a beach lying prone in the sun,
Bone-white, roughly licked carnivore-clean.

Bristling grass roughens the path.
Small, strange plants; slicing whipgrass,
Grey succulents with swollen fingers
Among the flayed ends of blue twine, burnt sticks.
A life of fighting the sickening, shrivelling salt.

The alcohol of the white air –
Unseen gulls reduce to sharp cries on a falling curve
Over the spongy edge of the cliff,
Streaking down to the sprung tightness of the water;
Hard glances bouncing off its strolling skin,
Paisleyed by the skidding wind.

Bright and dark verdigris stain the sandy bed.
Dark clumps growing deep, shifting their weight and swaying
On a strong, slow current.
Piebald patches on the inner skin of the sea.

A high shadow wings and wheels in silence,
Hanging cruciform in the thermal drift.
There's a hole seared in the shadow where the eye would be,
It scorches the ground. Rabbits ping into the scrub
With the low-to-the ground speed of real terror.

The breeze drops again, drops like a gift into the lap
The cracked bell of the waves.